In memory of Alice Sears McGee and in honor of
my darling grandson Benton Ray Min – M. M.

For my dear friends Tee and Tree!
With BIG thanks – C. B.

LITTLE TIGER PRESS LTD,
an imprint of the Little Tiger Group
1 Coda Studios, 189 Munster Road, London SW6 6AW
www.littletiger.co.uk

First published in Great Britain 2010
This edition published 2013

Text copyright © Marni McGee 2010
Illustrations copyright © Cee Biscoe 2010

Marni McGee and Cee Biscoe have asserted their rights
to be identified as the author and illustrator of this work under
the Copyright, Designs and Patents Act, 1988

All rights reserved • ISBN 978-1-4351-4763-8

Printed in China

Lot #: 2 4 6 8 10 9 7 5 3
12/17

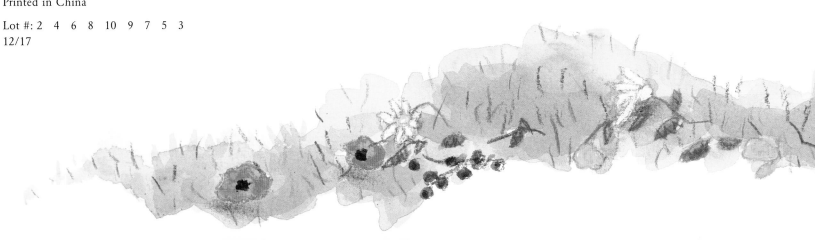

Bumble

The Little Bear With BIG Ideas!

Marni McGee

Cee Biscoe

Bumble splashed across the stream then trotted up the hill. Grandma would be waiting — with cakes and cups of tea served with lots of honey.

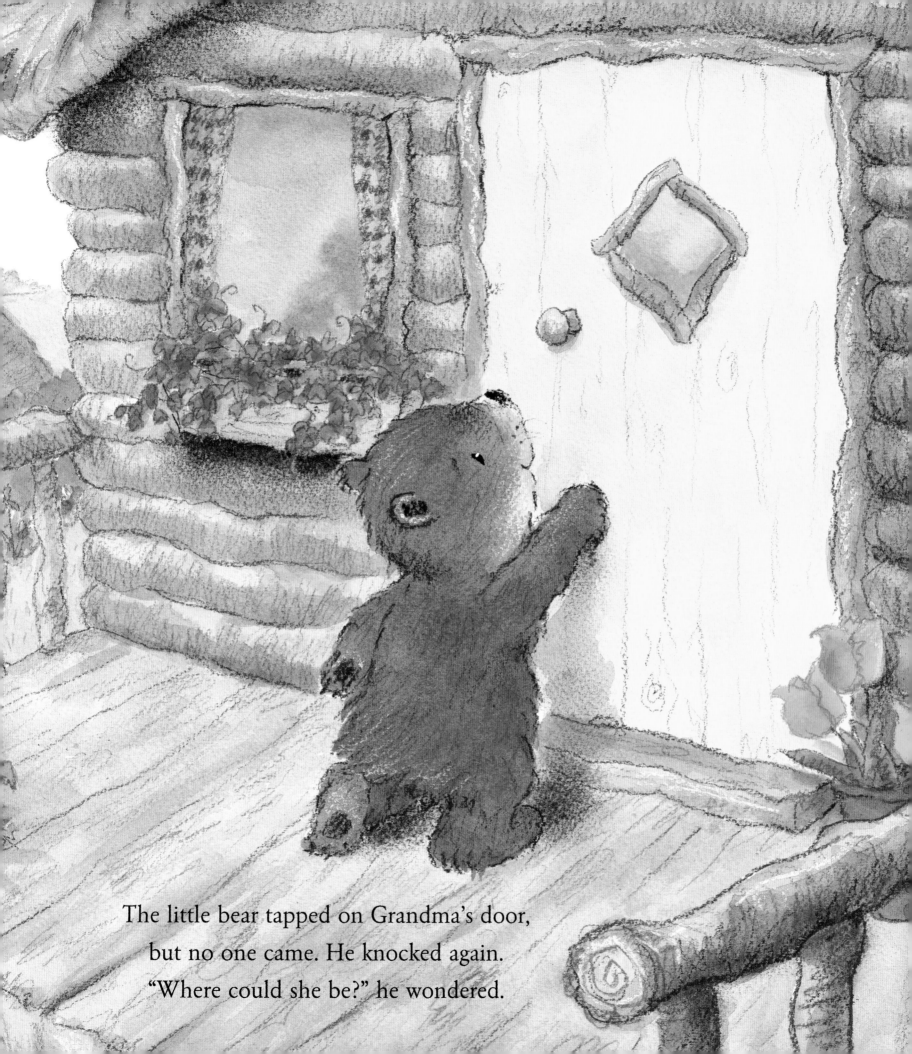

The little bear tapped on Grandma's door,
but no one came. He knocked again.
"Where could she be?" he wondered.

Three forest birds flew down.
"Quiet," said Crow.
"She's sleeping, you know."

"She couldn't be sleeping," Bumble declared.
"Grandma Bear is waiting for me!"
"Not true," Owl hooted. "Bear set out
for honey. She tripped on a root."

"Hit her head,"
cawed Hawk.
"I saw."

"My grandma fell down?" gasped Bumble. He peered
in the window. Sure enough, Grandma was asleep,
with a big lump on her head. "Poor Grandma!"
Bumble cried.

Then he had an idea.
"Grandma loves flowers," he said.

He ran to the garden and picked
the flowers there —
every single one.

Bumble smiled as he tiptoed past Grandma.
He put flowers in vases, jars, buckets,
and bowls and set them all over the room.
"She will be SO surprised!" he whispered.

"Now what should I do next?"
the little bear wondered.
He saw four pots of paint.

"I know!" he exclaimed.
"I'll paint the door for Grandma."
    At first he could not choose:
should he paint with red or yellow,
blue or grassy green?

In the end, he used . . .

. . . ALL of the colors!

He painted a picture on Grandma's front door.

Bumble smiled again. "She will be SO surprised!"

Bumble saw dirty dishes in the sink. He washed them
very carefully, saving Grandma's favorite cup till last —
a cup so fine, its rim was trimmed with gold.

Bumble held his breath as he washed that cup . . .
held his breath as he rinsed.

But just then the forest birds came back,
squawking. What if they woke up Grandma?
Bumble began to hurry.

Bumble grabbed a cloth to dry. The cup slipped.
It seemed to **fly**.

Bumble reached to catch it,

but he missed.

Grandma's cup fell.

CRASH!

Bumble **ran.** He stumbled to the door, tumbled out and hid.

"Just **look** what that Bumble has done!" fussed Owl.

"He stripped her garden **bare!**" squawked Hawk.

"Grandma Bear will be **angry**, you know," said Crow.

Bumble heard footsteps on the porch.
He peeped through the railings . . .

. . . Grandma Bear was **there!**

"Bumble did it **all,**" cawed Hawk.
"I saw!"

Bumble took a big breath and crawled out. "I wanted to surprise you," he said.

"You **did** surprise me, Bumble Bear," said Grandma,
"but the birds are wrong. I **like** my beautiful door!"
And she shooed the forest birds away.

"I picked all of your flowers," Bumble wailed.
Grandma just shrugged. "We will plant some more."

The little bear gulped. "But Grandma, that's not all. I broke your favorite cup, the one with the glitter-gold rim."

"My cup?" she gasped. "There's not another one like it, not anywhere else in the world." A tear slid down poor Bumble's nose.

"But that is true of you, dear Bumble, too!
There is not another bear like you, not
anywhere else in the world. You are
the best little bear in the forest!"

Bumble smiled. "Should I make us some tea?"
Grandma pulled him close. "Let's
make it **together.**"

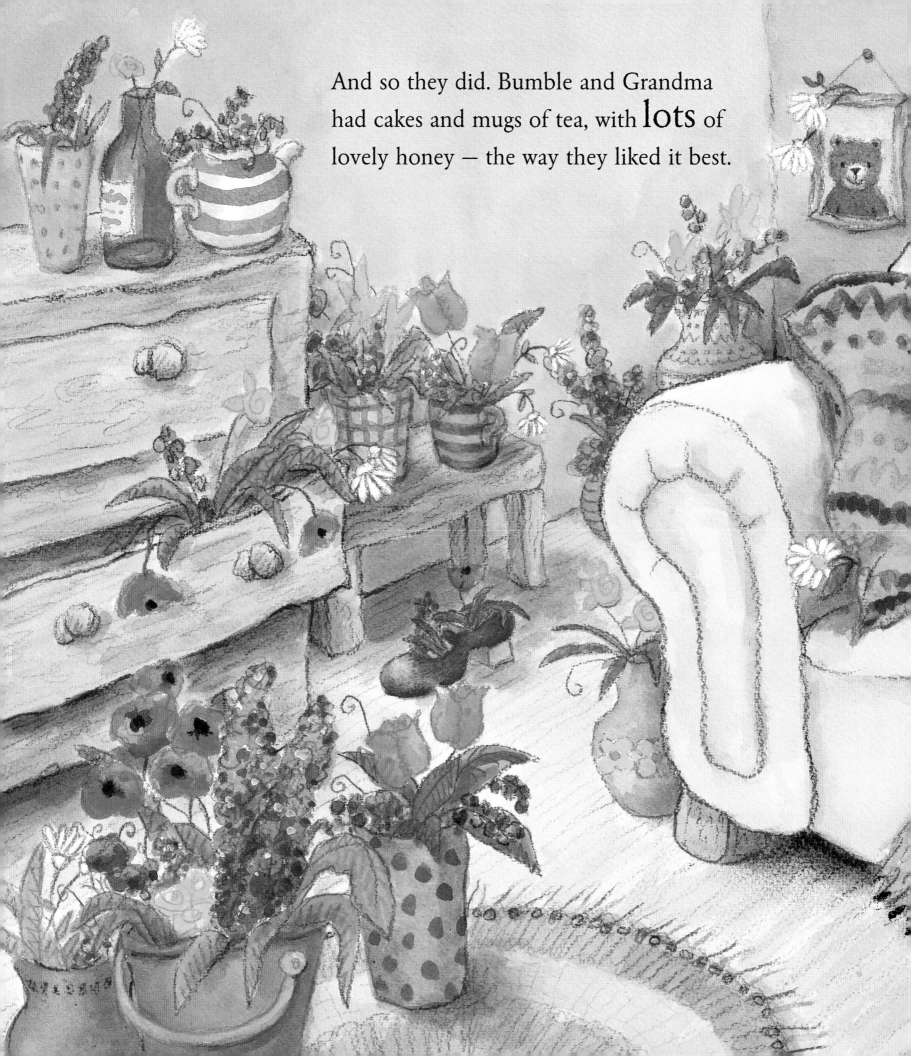

And so they did. Bumble and Grandma had cakes and mugs of tea, with lots of lovely honey — the way they liked it best.